First published in Great Britain in 1984
under the imprint Abelard/North-South by Abelard-
Schuman Ltd and reprinted in 1985 by North-South Books,
an imprint of Rada Matija AG and reprinted in 1987.
First published in the United States in 1985 by North-South Books,
an imprint of Rada Matija AG and reprinted in 1987.

Distributed in the United States by
Henry Holt and Company, Inc., 521 Fifth Avenue,
New York, New York 10175.
Library of Congress Cataloging in Publication Data

Miller, his son, and their donkey. English.
The miller, his son, and their donkey.

Published in Switzerland under the title: Der Muller,
sein Sohn und ihr Esel.
Summary: A miller and his son, on their way to market
with their donkey, find it impossible to please everyone they meet.
[1. Fables]   I. Aesop.   II. Sopko, Eugen, ill.
III. Title.
PZ8.2.M55   1985   398.2'1   [E]   85-7198
ISBN 0-8050-0475-0

Distributed in Great Britain by
Blackie and Son Ltd, 7 Leicester Place,
London WC2H 7BP.
British Library Cataloguing in Publication Data

Lanning, Rosemary
The miller, his son and their donkey.
I. Title   II. Sopko, Eugen
823'.914[J]   PZ7
ISBN 0-200-72846-6

Distributed in Australia and New Zealand by
Buttercup Books Pty. Ltd., Melbourne.
ISBN 0 949447 47 1

Printed in Germany

A FABLE FROM AESOP

The Miller, His Son and Their Donkey

Pictures by EUGEN SOPKO

North-South Books
New York   London   Melbourne

One day a miller set off for the market, riding his donkey. His son came walking along behind him.

Soon they met a musician. "What an unkind father you are!" he said. "How can you make the poor boy walk while you ride? You're bigger and stronger than him." So the miller and his son changed places.

After a while they met a farm worker, eating his lunch. "You lazy boy!" he said. "Fancy you riding and making your poor old father walk. You've got younger legs!"

So the miller climbed on to the donkey's back and father and son both rode for a mile or so. Then they met an old man who shouted at them, "How can you be so cruel to that donkey? Two people on one poor, weak animal! Get down at once, or I'll knock you down with my stick!"

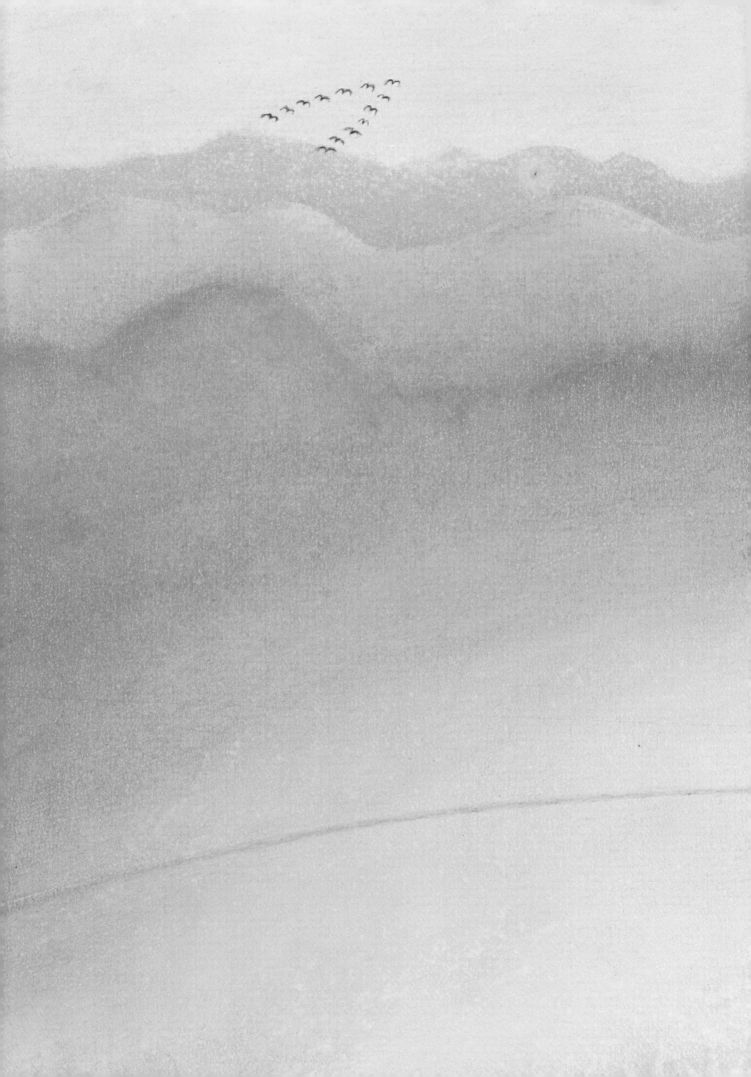

So they both got down and
all three walked for a stretch, with the
father on the right, the son on the left
and the donkey in the middle.

Then they met a traveller. He laughed when he saw them. "What funny fellows you are!" he said. "Why should all three of you walk when one could ride?"

So the miller and his son
tied the donkey's legs together and
carried him between them, slung from a
strong branch.

But that was so
uncomfortable for the donkey that he
wrenched himself free and kicked both
the miller and his son so hard . . .

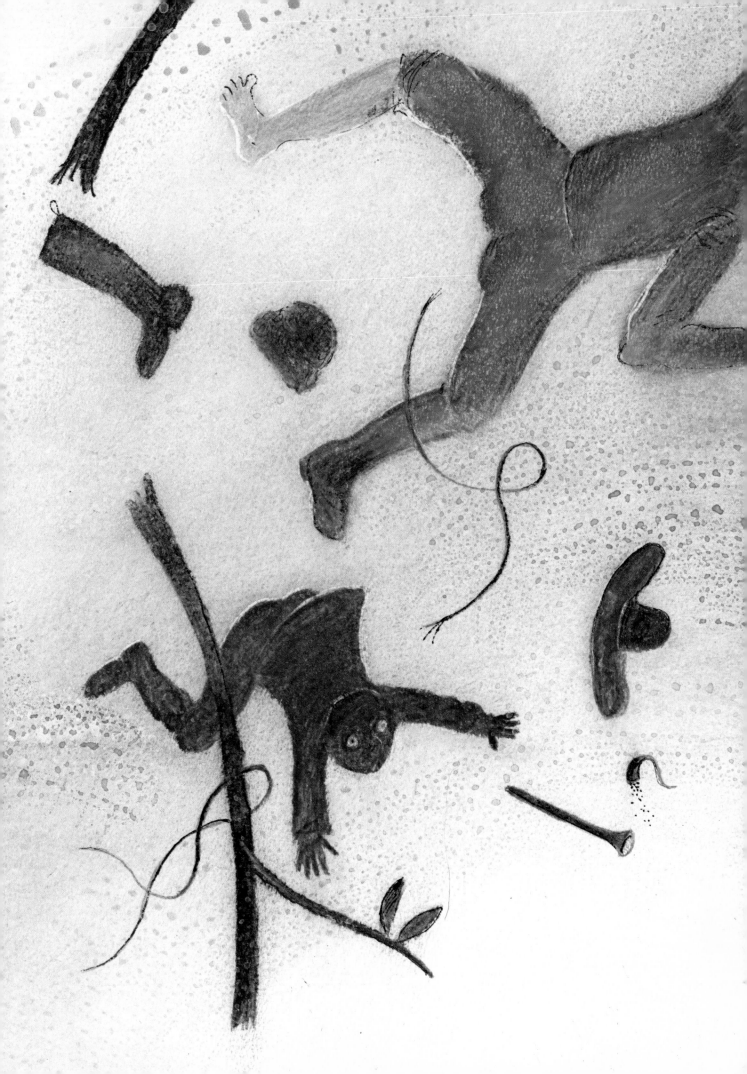

. . . that the son flew right up in the air and came down in a mud pit and the father landed face down in a heap of straw.

Happy at last, the donkey
kicked up its heels and trotted away.

MORAL:

*You can
never please
everyone.*